THE
MORNING
GLORY

THE
MORNING
GLORY

PROSE POEMS BY

ROBERT BLY

HARPER & ROW, PUBLISHERS
NEW YORK, EVANSTON
SAN FRANCISCO, LONDON

I am grateful to the editors of the following magazines who published some of these poems in their magazines: *Kayak, Crazy Horse, Apple, Modern Occasions, Knife River Press, Café Solo, The Iowa Review, Hearse, Dragonfly, It, New York Quarterly, Panjandrum, Tennessee Poetry Journal,* Tony Petrosky's *Broadside Series, Isthmus, New Letters, Chicago Review, Clear Creek, Choice, Peace and Pieces, Sceptre Press, Tempest, UT Review, Field, Sadvipra, Madrona,* and *Poetry.*

Twenty of these poems were published earlier in *The Morning Glory,* published by Kayak Press, copyright © 1969–1970 by Robert Bly. Thanks to George Hitchcock for permission to republish them here.

"Leonardo's Secret" was printed in the prose section of *Sleepers Joining Hands.* Copyright © 1973 by Robert Bly, Harper & Row.

"The Hockey Poem" originally appeared in *The Ohio Review.*

The section called "The Point Reyes Poems" was published earlier by Mudra Press as a pamphlet called "Point Reyes Poems," and I am grateful to Mudra Press for permission to reprint them here.

FIRST EDITION

Designed by *Janice Willcocks Stern*

Library of Congress Cataloging in Publication Data

Bly, Robert.
   The morning glory.
   I. Title.
PS3552.L9M6   811'.5'4   74–15811
ISBN 0–06–010368–X
ISBN 0–06–010367–1 pbk.

---

75 76 77 78 79 10 9 8 7 6 5 4 3 2 1

For Mary
who brought me a gift

Contents

I.

II.
The Point Reyes Poems

III.

There is an old occult saying: whoever wants to see the invisible has to penetrate more deeply into the visible. All through Taoist and "curving lines" thought, there is the idea that our disasters come from letting nothing live for itself, from the longing we have to pull everything, even friends, in to ourselves, and let nothing alone. If we examine a pine carefully, we see how independent it is of us. When we first sense that a pine tree really doesn't need us, that it has a physical life and a moral life and a spiritual life that is complete without us, we feel alienated and depressed. The second time we feel it, we feel joyful. As Basho says in his wonderful poem:

> The morning glory—
> another thing
> that will never be my friend.

I

A Bird's Nest Made of
White Reed Fiber

The nest is white as the foam thrown up when the sea hits rocks! It is translucent as those cloudy transoms above Victorian doors, and swirled as the hair of those intense nurses, gray and tangled after long nights in Crimean wards. It is something made and then forgotten, like our own lives that we will entirely forget in the grave, when we are floating, nearing the shore where we will be reborn, ecstatic and black.

Leonardo's Secret

(THE VIRGIN AND ST. ANNE)

The Virgin is thinking of a child—who will drive the rioters out of the Temple—and her face is smiling. Her smile is full, it reminds you of a cow's side, or a stubble field with water standing in it.

Behind her head, jagged blue rocks. The pointed rocks slope up quietly, and fall back, washed by a blue light, like the light in an octopus's eyes. The rocks, though no one is there, are not empty of people.

The rocks have not been forgotten by the sea either. They are the old brains of the sea. They glow for several seconds every morning, as the old man who lives in a hut on the shore drinks down his glass of saltwater.

Looking at a Dead Wren
in My Hand

Forgive the hours spent listening to radios, and the words of gratitude I did not say to teachers. I love your tiny rice-like legs, that are bars of music played in an empty church, and the feminine tail, where no worms of Empire have ever slept, and the intense yellow chest that makes tears come. Your tail feathers open like a picket fence, and your bill is brown, with the sorrow of an old Jew whose daughter has married an athlete. The black spot on your head is your own mourning cap.

Sitting on Some Rocks
in Shaw Cove, California

I am in a cliff-hollow, surrounded by fossils and furry shells. The sea breathes and breathes under the new moon. Suddenly it rises, hurrying into the long crevices in the rock shelves, it rises like a woman's belly, as if nine months had passed in a second; rising like milk to the tiny veins, it overflows like a snake going over a low wall.

I have the sensation that half an inch under my skin there are nomad bands, stringy-legged men with fire-sticks and wide-eyed babies. The rocks with their backs turned to me have something spiritual in them. On these rocks I am not afraid of death; death is like the sound of the motor in an airplane as we fly, the sound so steady and comforting. And I still haven't found the woman I loved in some former life—how could I, when I have loved only once on this rock, though twice in the moon, and three times in the rising water. Two children a thousand miles away leap toward me, shouting, arms in the air. A bird with long wings comes flying toward me in the dusk, pumping just over the darkening waves. He has flown around the whole planet, it has taken him centuries. He returns to me the lean-legged runner laughing as he runs through the stringy grasses, and gives back to me my buttons, and the soft sleeves of my sweater.

At a Fish Hatchery in
Story, Wyoming

A ranger is lifting fingerling trout from a pickup with his scoop. They are weighing the fingerlings for stocking. The man in black boots pours them out of his scoop into a tub set on a scale. The fish slip off the scoop shovel, five or six inches long, shiny, gleaming, full of life! How they twist and turn in the Wyoming sun, about to fall! They are immense reserves of pure energy, like snowbanks, like mountains, like millions of hands . . . and when they do fall, they leave behind pure strokes in the air, vanishing into the washtub of fish, that contains so much, like the white stones dropped by glaciers, and washed by chilly streams . . . or the furs wrapped around old shoulders in the back of caves, where the skins have been chewed by women with luminous faces, who glow because their child has come into the universe . . . and now lies on their naked breast, which gleams in the risen light like a fish.

The Hunter

I hear a ticking on the Pacific stones. A white shape is moving in the furry air of the seacoast. The moon narrow, the sea quiet. He comes closer, a long time the stick ticks on over the rock faces. Is it a postal employee saddened by the sleet? It comes nearer. I talk. The shape talks, it is a Japanese man carrying a spear and a heavy-bellied little bag. The spear has a hook on the end. What are you looking for, clams? No! Octopus!
Did you get any? I found three. He sits down. I get up and walk over. May I see them? He opens the plastic bag. I turn on the flashlight. Something wet, fantastic, womblike, horse-intestine-like. May I take hold of one? His voice smiles. Why not? I reach in. Dry things stick to my hands, like burrs from burdocks, compelling, pleading, dry, poor, in debt. You boil them, then sauté them. I look and cannot find the eyes. He is a cook. He ate them in Japan.
So the octopus is gone now from the mussel-ridden

shelf with the low roof, the pool where he waited under the thin moon, but the sea never came back, no one came home, the door never opened. Now he is taken away in the plastic bag, not understood, illiterate.

A Hollow Tree

I bend over an old hollow cottonwood stump, still standing, waist high, and look inside. Early spring. Its Siamese temple walls are all brown and ancient. The walls have been worked on by the intricate ones. Inside the hollow walls there is privacy and secrecy, dim light. And yet some creature has died here.

On the temple floor feathers, gray feathers, many of them with a fluted white tip. Many feathers. In the silence many feathers.

Looking into a Tide Pool

It is a tide pool, shallow, water coming in, clear, tiny white shell-people on the bottom, asking nothing, not even directions! On the surface the noduled seaweed, lying like hands, slowly drawing back and returning, hands laid on fevered bodies, moving back and forth, as the healer sings wildly, shouting to Jesus and his dead mother.